WWII
D-Day Landings

Liam McCann

WWII
D-Day Landings

First published in the UK in 2014

© Demand Media Limited 2014

www.demand-media.co.uk

Printed and bound in Europe

ISBN 978-1-909768-59-8

Contents

Introduction

By 1940 British forces had been ejected from northern France, although the heroic evacuation at Dunkirk saved 300,000 men from the advancing Germans. Instead of trying to take back the ground conceded, Churchill diverted his remaining resources to North Africa and only returned to France with the Americans on D-Day in 1944. During these four years, Stalin's Russia bore the brunt of the conflict with the Nazis on the terrible Eastern Front.

Having been brought into the war by the Japanese in late 1941, Roosevelt believed that the fight in Europe should be targeted directly at Germany across the English Channel, but the Americans were newcomers to the war

and Churchill convinced them to attack easier targets in North Africa and the Mediterranean, what he called Hitler's soft underbelly. Roosevelt went along with the plan initially but he privately pressured Churchill to reconsider from as early as 1942.

And this so-called underbelly wasn't as soft as Churchill believed. Indeed it wasn't long before Allied troops were bogged down in a war of attrition against a determined enemy fighting for every island in the Mediterranean and every square mile of the Sahara Desert. The Red Army, on the other hand, was at last making progress on the Eastern Front and was heading for the real prize: Berlin. So why did Churchill continue to concentrate on the Mediterranean instead of helping the Russians by splitting German forces in central Europe?

There's no doubt that the preservation of empire and a fear of a return to trench warfare in the north of France played a role in his decision, but there was more to it than that. Churchill may have appeared resolute in the face of adversity during the retreat from Dunkirk and the Battle of Britain but

ABOVE The American tanker Gulfland is sunk by U-boats attacking the Atlantic convoys

FAR LEFT A line of British soldiers wades through water to a rescue ship off Dunkirk

INTRODUCTION

he was a leader under pressure who was aware that Britain, if the Atlantic blockade by German U-boats continued unchecked, would probably lose the war. The reality was that the conflict was exposing Churchill's soft underbelly.

When he received news that 33,000 men at Tobruk, a vital port in Libya, had surrendered after a daring German move to cut the city's supply lines in June 1942, he was mortified. Allied defences had been poorly maintained and the far smaller German army had taken advantage of low morale to force the British to capitulate. Churchill saw it as a disgrace but, more than that, it opened the way for Field Marshal Erwin Rommel to attack strategic targets like the Suez Canal in Egypt. Coming just after the fall of Singapore, when 90,000 Allied soldiers had surrendered to a vastly inferior Japanese force, it was another blow to British morale. More defeats in Norway, Greece and Crete heaped humiliation upon humiliation.

Conventional thinking at the beginning of the war was that Britain was still a global power because of its vast empire, but these disasters were weakening the country and were damaging for its leader. Churchill had fought on the frontiers in India, Sudan and South Africa and knew that protecting the empire was almost as important as defending the islands during the Battle of Britain.

When Italy joined the conflict on

Germany's side in June 1940, Churchill felt even more threatened in the Mediterranean. Mussolini could call upon a powerful navy, and Italy already had colonies in Africa, so, if he could brush the British aside in Libya and Egypt before taking Cairo, that would be the coup de grâce for the British Empire.

Churchill had to counter the Italian threat and desperately needed morale-boosting victories so he ordered half his tanks to Egypt, his priority being to pre-serve the empire's supply lines through the Suez Canal. These supply lines guaranteed oil from the Persian Gulf and troops from India and Australasia, without which the British war effort would falter.

Mussolini's optimism was misplaced and he overestimated his army's ability to fight a desert campaign. The British counterattacked during Operation Compass under Major-General Richard O'Connor, driving deep into Libya and routing the retreating Italians. It seemed that Churchill's gamble would pay off.

Hitler was so concerned about taking the canal that he sent Rommel, the Desert Fox, to Libya with divisions of tanks and elite troops in February 1941. Rommel was an unconventional

but tactically astute leader who often ignored instructions from the High Command and repeatedly outmanoeuvred the British. His Afrika Korps would attack unexpectedly and gradually pushed a British Eighth Army – weakened after sending reinforcements to Greece – back towards Cairo. Despite counterattacks by both sides, by early 1942 Britain had ceded Benghazi and Gazala and much of western Egypt, and their position in North Africa was once again on a knife-edge.

Churchill had been concentrating on beefing up the air force and navy, and this led to under-funding and chronic shortages within the army, which was now the weakest it had been since the Great War. The prime minister had to save face so he launched a massive recruitment drive. Soldiers needed to be trained in the art of desert warfare so they could take on Rommel, but they were young and inexperienced, and so were their commanders. Chief of the Imperial General Staff Sir Alan Brooke even went as far as saying that half of the entire military wing was unfit for purpose. He blamed the inadequacies on the First World War, which had robbed this generation of their most tal-

ented officers. To cap it all, Churchill's leadership was now being questioned and he had to fend off two votes of no confidence in the House of Commons.

As if this wasn't bad enough, the colonies now began to question British rule. Future Chancellor Stafford Cripps had already drawn up plans to give India independence, and Egypt was also clamouring for the end of imperial rule from London. Rommel, in fact, was looked upon as a liberator.

The British reacted with heavy hands: Ambassador Sir Miles Lampson marched into King Farouk's palace and demanded that he form a pro-British Egyptian government or abdicate. Farouk chose the former, although Egypt officially remained neutral until the last year of the war, by which time the fighting had long-since ceased.

It seemed that only a decisive British victory in the desert could save the empire. Instead, the humiliation at Tobruk seemed to have sealed its fate and Churchill began to unravel. His only hope now lay with nurturing a special relationship with the Americans.

ABOVE The bodies of Canadian servicemen litter the beach after the disastrous raid on Dieppe in 1942

FAR LEFT Sir Alan Brooke

ABOVE Wounded Canadians shelter near an abandoned Churchill tank while one of the landing craft burns in the background

His first priority, however, was to fly to Africa and sack the commanders who had allowed Rommel to within striking distance of Cairo. He replaced them with General Bernard Montgomery, a man determined to toughen up the troops and take no more backward steps. Montgomery's confidence and informality endeared him to the rank and file, and by October 1942 the army was ready to attack Rommel's inferior force at Alamein.

Montgomery was also fortified with news from Britain's decoders at Bletchley Park. They had broken the German Enigma Code and knew where and when to find German convoys re-supplying Rommel, as well as his tank movements in the desert. On 23rd October 1942, Montgomery launched his artillery bombardment. Instead of securing quick victory with an overwhelming number of tanks, however, the British were forced to pick their way through enormous minefields, and the battle soon turned into an infantry arm-wrestle which hung in the balance for nearly two weeks. In the final reckoning, it was Rommel who conceded defeat and ended up in retreat. This was the British army's first victory over the Germans, and it guaranteed Churchill's position for the rest of the war.

He called it the decisive land battle of the conflict, but this was merely rhetoric to boost morale. The reality was that the British had lost more men in the engagement and Montgomery's cautious pursuit allowed Rommel and the majority of his Afrika Korps to escape (they would eventually be redeployed to the second front in Northern France). The Americans were not impressed with either the motive for the campaign or the outcome. They believed it was a selfish attempt by the British to cling on to colonial power when the real fight lay against Hitler in Europe.

As early as April 1942 General George Marshall visited Britain to outline his plans for the second front. The British were unconvinced by his timeta-

ble – he wanted to launch the attack by Christmas – but praised Marshall's boldness and promised to go along with the plan, with one important reservation: they had to be allowed to continue their defence of India and the

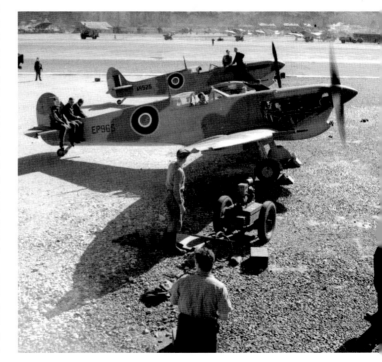

ABOVE Stalin, Roosevelt and Churchill convene in Tehran in 1943

Middle East. Churchill was clearly still the senior partner in the alliance but power was shifting perceptibly to the Americans. The prime minister was also concerned that the US would only be able to contribute a couple of divisions to the new front if they moved in 1942, so the majority of the troops would have to come from the Commonwealth, notably Canada.

A lightning raid on the Channel port of Dieppe in late 1942 showed just how fragile the Allies were. The Canadians lost seventy percent of their men during the disastrous assault. It proved to be a costly but ultimately worthwhile lesson because it dissuaded the Americans from going ahead with an all-out attack, a campaign they would surely have lost. It also brought home the difficulties of landing men and machinery in a heavily defended port.

Churchill therefore found it easy to convince the Americans and Russians that France was Hitler's tough snout, whereas a second front in Italy would continue striking at his soft under-belly. The thinking was that the British army would have more luck against the weaker Italian military, and defeating Mussolini would ensure the security of the British Empire.

Marshall wasn't sure but he wasn't prepared to overrule Churchill by going behind his back to Roosevelt. The president was facing hostility at home from a people who wanted peace with Hitler so they could concentrate on avenging Pearl Harbor. He desperately needed American blood to be shed in direct conflict with the Nazis so that the country would unite against the Axis Powers. Roosevelt therefore gave the green light to Operation Torch, an invasion of North Africa that would trap the retreating Rommel.

Churchill let him select the com-mander for the operation, so Roosevelt chose Dwight Eisenhower because he had a better relationship with the British officers. It was the biggest amphibious assault to date, dwarfing the Gallipoli landings during the First World War. The initial advances were positive and the Allies confidently predicted that they'd oust Rommel from the continent by Christmas.

Hitler had other ideas, however. He rushed troops and supplies into Tunisia so Rommel could make a last stand. In one engagement at the Kasserine Pass, the new American recruits were routed and driven back 85 miles in a week. Churchill and Brooke were now more determined than ever to end the campaign in North Africa before striking at Italy, but Marshall didn't believe the war could be won here. Churchill overruled him and was finally vindicated with the capture of Tunis in early 1943. They took a dozen German generals and 250,000 men prisoner, but the victory came six months after Stalingrad and the Axis soon recovered.

Marshall again lobbied for the second front in France, but Churchill knew they still didn't have the men or resources to mount the offensive so the Americans beach-hopped across the Mediterranean instead. The landings at Sicily proved just how fragile their alliance was, how-ever. They lost 20,000 men in the first month and the relationship between Montgomery and his American counterparts, George Patton in particular, almost reached breaking point.

They managed to stay civil until Sicily fell, by which time Mussolini's fascists were about to be overthrown. The new leadership surrendered and tried to join the Allies but, instead of being able to draw on their support, Montgomery and Patton were pitched against German forces in the north.

With the Americans still pushing for the second front, Churchill decided to shore up Italian defences, secure the Balkans, take the islands in the Aegean, intensify the bombing campaign against Germany and, lastly, build up American troops in Britain in preparation for the future invasion of France. In other words, the second front was still bottom of his list of priorities.

The code-breakers at Bletchley Park had intelligence that once the Allies had a firm hold in Italy, the Germans would retreat north. This would give the Allies room to strike at the industrial centres in southern Germany. But Hitler again surprised them by standing firm in Rome and drawing them into a war of attrition. They also fought a guerrilla-style campaign in the mountains and kept the Allies at bay for the winter of 1943-44.

Churchill had expected an easy time in the Aegean but the German defence was again resolute. Brooke believed the prime minister was spreading his forces too thinly around the islands when Italy needed to be finished off. Marshall and Roosevelt backed him up and informed Churchill that Operation Overlord would take place with or without his consent in the spring of 1944.

Churchill, Roosevelt and Stalin met in Tehran in 1943 in tense circumstances. Stalin's Red Army was pushing the Germans back through the Ukraine and the Americans were finally making progress in the Far East. Churchill was under pressure as never before. Roosevelt and Stalin insisted that the Allies struck in France, so Churchill was again outvoted. With Russia and America fully mobilised, he was increasingly marginalised as the junior partner and this filled him with resentment. On the return journey to London he suffered two minor heart attacks.

During his recovery, he decided to launch a final offensive in Italy to convince Stalin and Roosevelt that Britain

ABOVE The ruins of
Monte Cassino

was still a force. The landings at Anzio were successful but the troops failed to press home their advantage and were soon pinned down by German bombers. The sides slugged it out in particularly brutal engagements such as at the German-held monastery of Monte Cassino.

Despite taking severe casualties, the Allied bombers eventually levelled the monastery, but the Germans fought on for five months in the rubble. It was akin to the Somme in its brutality but the Germans finally capitulated. General Mark Clark's Fifth Army then broke out from the beachhead and liberated Rome, but his moment in the spotlight was overshadowed when the Allies launched Overlord in Normandy the following day.

Operation Overlord

Churchill had long been opposed to landing men on the beaches of Normandy – he'd been partly responsible for the disastrous Gallipoli landings in World War One – but he was eventually talked into agreeing Operation Neptune (the landings themselves) as part of the broader Operation Overlord.

The Americans had been pushing for a second front against the Nazis in France but Churchill was so concerned about the strength of his army that he convinced Roosevelt to attack German and Italian forces in North Africa and the Mediterranean instead. By 1944, however, he could no longer keep the Americans out of Europe. Indeed Operation Sledgehammer (1942) and the larger Operation Roundup (1943) had already been shelved, and the Americans believed time was running out.

Roundup was adapted into Overlord,

which was discussed by the Allied leaders at conferences in Casablanca and Quebec in 1943. The upshot was that British and American forces would "establish a foothold in Northern France before striking at the heart of Germany to destroy her military forces". Planning the assault gathered momentum after the Tehran Conference later that year, by which time Lieutenant-General Frederick Morgan and American Major General Ray Barker had assumed command (under the acronym COSSAC – Chief of Staff to the Supreme Allied Commander).

They immediately encountered problems with a seaborne assault, however: Churchill's insistence on capturing Greek and Italian islands in the Mediterranean had left the Allies short of landing craft; and the disastrous raid on Dieppe in 1942, which led to nearly 4,000 Canadians being killed or captured by an inferior German force, proved that landing men and machinery on a well-defended beachhead was practically suicidal.

There were more constraints on the site of the landings themselves because Allied fighters like the Spitfire and

ABOVE The 3D stereoscopic images of the Normandy coast are analysed by British Intelligence

Typhoon had relatively short ranges. To have any chance of success, the beach assault would need air cover for as long as possible. When the geography of the French coast was analysed, only two landing sites were found to be suitable: the Pas de Calais and the Normandy coast.

The sites had their own pros and cons. The Pas de Calais was closer to

ABOVE Allied supply ships approach Mulberry B off Gold Beach

Germany and was to the north of the Seine, which would give the Allies fewer obstacles. The area was extremely well fortified by Hitler's Atlantic Wall, however, and many smaller rivers and canals would still have to be crossed. If the assault went well and the German army was forced to retreat, they could destroy key bridges across the waterways to hinder the Allied advance.

The Normandy beaches weren't as well defended but the main port, Cherbourg, was well to the west and did house a massive German presence. An attack here would still leave the Allies having to cross the Seine, although if they landed at several beaches they would be able to push inland towards Paris and Germany simultaneously. Morgan and Baker presented various proposals at the Quebec Conference and Normandy was eventually chosen, with a provisional date of May 1st 1944.

On December 31st 1943, Supreme Allied Commander General Dwight D Eisenhower, General Bernard

Montgomery and Winston Churchill were presented with the draft plans while in Morocco. They raised concerns about the scale of the attack and suggested expanding the invasion to five beaches and 39 divisions, or more than a million men in total.

On the same night, torpedo boats of the Royal Engineers under Major Logan Scott-Bowden surveyed the beaches, with he and Sergeant Bruce Ogden-Smith actually swimming ashore to collect soil samples. The land beyond the beaches was known to be boggy so the samples were essential for evaluating whether the ground could support tanks and artillery. During the next few days, the submarine HMS X20 under Lieutenant-Commander Ken Hudspeth continued surveying the beaches, while at night Scott-Bowden's men swam ashore at various points to complete

BELOW Mulberry A was destroyed during a storm that raged from June 19-22

their mission. (Hudspeth's X20 would later act as a navigation beacon guiding men and equipment ashore on Juno Beach, action for which he was awarded a DSC.)

The next phase of the operation involved reconnaissance of the beaches and the villages inland, so the BBC launched an appeal for people to send in their holiday photos of the area for a mock exhibition. Unarmed RAF Spitfires also flew sorties over the coast with multiple stereoscopic cameras on each aircraft so that a 3D mosaic of the terrain could be produced. This new photographic technique allowed the Allies to examine the pictures in greater detail, picking out previously unknown gun emplacements, minefields and bunkers.

The public response and the results of these surveys were then used to create two detailed scale topographical maps of the beaches. One was given to the War Department at the Metropole Hotel while Churchill had the second delivered to the Cabinet War Rooms. The terrain was then reproduced with great accuracy at Cairnryan in Scotland so that the planners could test various methods of landing men and machinery on the beaches. The peat bogs behind

ABOVE These vast conundrums were used to lay the PLUTO

FAR LEFT The PLUTO being laid

the Normandy beaches gave COSSAC the greatest concern so they planned to use spools of heavy-duty matting to cover the most sodden ground.

Montgomery then outlined the invasion itself, with the main objectives in the opening exchanges being to secure the beaches, take Cherbourg with its deep-water port, liberate Brittany with all of its harbours, and advance towards Paris from Le Havre. He foresaw the town of Caen as pivotal because securing the area would open up an advance to Paris. If Cherbourg couldn't be

taken, Montgomery knew the Allies would have to rely on the other ports, and if that wasn't possible, they'd have to make their own.

The prefabricated Mulberry harbour and pipeline under the ocean (PLUTO) were therefore designed and built to help the invasion. The failed raid on Dieppe had shown how difficult it would be to breach the Atlantic Wall and secure a big port, essential if men and supplies were to be offloaded throughout the D-Day landings. The Mulberry harbours were designed so that troops

and cargo could be rapidly deployed to support Overlord. In just three days after the first landings, Mulberry A and B – at Omaha Beach and Arromanches respectively – had been built. Mulberry A was destroyed in a storm two weeks later but Mulberry B was used for the rest of the year and is reckoned to have allowed four million tons of supplies and nearly three million men to be deployed in Northern France.

The vast amount of machinery needed to be fuelled, hence the second innovation: several specially developed oil pipelines were laid under the Channel. The project was so big and complex that merchant ships had to be adapted to carry the mild-steel pipes. After small-scale tests were successful in the Firth of Clyde, HMS Holdfast was equipped with the rolling gear and 30 miles of pipe was laid across the Bristol Channel. The operation again ran smoothly and the pipelines were deployed in Normandy throughout the invasion. By March 1945 they were delivering a million gallons of fuel per day to the Allies.

As the invasion drew nearer, the Allies were understandably concerned that German spies in Britain would get

wind of it and Erwin Rommel, recalled from North Africa, would beef up the German defences along the Atlantic Wall. It was extremely difficult to lay all the pipeline, manufacture the hardware, run several mock beach assaults and gather millions of men, hundreds of ships and thousands of tons of military hardware without being spotted by German aerial reconnaissance aircraft or coming to the attention of their agents in the UK. Deceptions were needed to divert their attention.

Operation Bodyguard spread disinformation about possible landings in the South of France and the Balkans. Operation Fortitude then hinted at two possible assaults, the first in the strategically important but well-defended Pas de Calais, and the second in Norway. General Lesley McNair and Lieutenant-General George Patton were placed in charge of the fictional First US Army Group, and the Germans were fed further disinformation in the form of pointless radio traffic and messages from double agents. Indeed The Double-Cross System was an extremely effective tool for spreading rumours and misinformation as all of the

ABOVE Inflatable tanks were used to confuse the Germans about where the D-Day Landings would take place

FAR LEFT General Lesley McNair

ABOVE A dummy
Douglas A-20 Havoc

FAR RIGHT Supreme
Allied Commander
General Dwight
Eisenhower

German agents operating in Britain at the time were eventually turned (bar one who committed suicide). They reported an enormous amount of information back to their handlers, all of which was utterly useless and which doubtless drew Rommel's forces away from Normandy and back to the Pas de Calais.

As it was all but impossible to conceal the build-up of men and equipment from German reconnaissance aircraft, the deception continued with the Allies massing enormous numbers of dummy tanks and landing craft – some wooden, others inflatable – and then erecting tent cities in the southeast. Allied ships

repeatedly bombarded the gun emplacements in the Pas de Calais to further confuse the German High Command. More redundant radio traffic convinced Hitler to retain several divisions in Norway that could have helped blunt the Allied advance further south.

There were more dummy raids along the coast in the Pas de Calais in the days before the invasion, and such was the success of the disinformation spread in the spring that Hitler refused to beef up his defences further west. The final part of the ruse saw heavy bombers from 617 and 218 Squadrons dropping aluminium strips over the Straits of Dover to convince German radar operators that there was a large invasion force gathering offshore. (The strips gave a return similar to a fleet of ships towing barrage balloons.)

The last consideration was the weather: a night with a full moon was preferable because it gave the glider pilots a better view of their navigational landmarks, and the spring tides gave the landing craft deeper water so they could avoid more submerged obstacles laid by the Germans. The full moon fell on June 6th but Eisenhower preferred the day before. The weather, however, which had been good in May then deteriorated and June 4th and 5th were unsuitable because of high winds and treacherous seas.

Although bad weather forced the Allies to delay the assault, there was a small window of opportunity during a break in the weather on 6th June 1944. Head of the navy Admiral Bertram Ramsay, commander of the Allied air forces Air Chief Marshal Sir Trafford Leigh-Mallory, commander of all the land forces General Bernard Montgomery, and Supreme Allied Commander General Eisenhower then took the decision to launch the invasion.

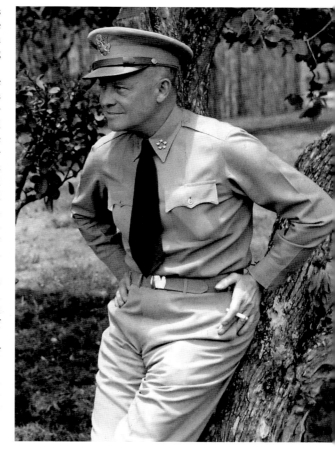

Chapter 2

Operation Tiger

Although the Allied preparations for D-Day appeared to have been well conceived and executed, they were not without their problems. In late 1943, the British government designated Slapton Sands in Devon as a training area because it was so similar to Utah Beach across the Channel. Several small exercises on the beach were followed by Operation Tiger in late April 1944.

Nine ships and 30,000 men were recruited to land on the sands and secure the beach. The Royal Navy was called in to shell the beach with live rounds so that the soldiers would get a more realistic appreciation of the sights and sounds and smells of action. General Eisenhower approved the live-fire exercise because most of the troops massing in southern England were not battle hardened and needed to experience a naval bombardment so that they weren't overawed when the real invasion began.

The embarkation and simulated Channel crossing phase of the operation went smoothly, and the troops were in their landing craft approaching the beach by first light on April 27th. The plan was for HMS Hawkins to shell the beach for half an hour, after which the sands would be inspected as a safety precaution before the landing craft came ashore.

Several of the landing craft were then slow getting into position so the commanding officer delayed the live-fire exercise by an hour. The message was

received by the crew of the Hawkins but not by some of the landing craft and they went ashore during the bombardment. As unpleasant and arduous as warfare can be, it is particularly galling when your own men are killed by friendly fire during a training exercise. Such was the confusion on the beach that a large contingent of American men breached the tape line beyond which they were not supposed to advance.

The support ships were then attacked by a patrol of nine German fast-attack E-boats. More confusion followed

ABOVE American troops come ashore on Slapton Sands during the Operation Tiger tragedy

ABOVE A German E-boat

FAR RIGHT The memorial to the Allied servicemen lost during the disaster

because British and American forces were operating on different radio frequencies. The E-boats targeted the tank landing ships (LSTs) and severely damaged or sunk four with the loss of 638 servicemen. Overall, the exercise resulted in the deaths of more than 1,000 troops, many of whom drowned because their lifejackets were fitted incorrectly and their backpacks flipped them face down into the water.

Such was the secrecy surrounding the beach assault that the figures weren't released until months later, by which time the incident had been largely forgotten because the main invasion was underway. Thankfully, some good did come out of the tragedy: radio frequencies were fixed to improve communication between support ships, destroyers and the landing craft; troops were better educated on how to use their lifejackets and where to balance their equipment; and contingency plans were made for rescuing servicemen stranded in the water.

Devon resident Ken Small wanted to commemorate the event but the British and American governments had no wish to erect a memorial to the victims. Small recruited a diving firm to help raise one of the Sherman tanks lost in the disaster, and it now stands as a permanent memorial to those who lost their lives.

Chapter 3

The Atlantic Wall

BELOW The German U-boat pens at Saint Nazaire

By early 1942 Hitler knew the Allies weren't in a position to launch a second front in Northern France for at least another year so he issued Fürher Directive 40 that called for the creation of the Atlantic Wall defences that would run from Norway in the north to Spain in the south. His resolve was stiffened when the Allies launched a successful commando raid on the submarine pens and dry dock at Saint Nazaire just south of Brest, putting the latter out of action for the remainder of the war. The raid convinced Hitler that German defences along thousands of miles of coastline needed to be upgraded.

ABOVE Conscripts protecting the Atlantic Wall

Organisation Todt had built the Siegfried defensive fortifications along the French-German border so they and thousands of forced labourers were drafted in to build permanent defences along the Atlantic coast. A year later Rommel inspected the wall but found it to be wholly inadequate so he drew up plans for a network of obstacles on the beaches themselves. They were usually

ABOVE German soldiers lay the obstacles that would so hamper the Allied landings

laid down in three rows around the tide line and consisted of dragon's teeth or hedgehogs (metallic obstructions), mines and wooden stakes. Further inland, concrete pillboxes lined the beaches; reinforced bunkers hid machine-gun nests, anti-tank positions and artillery batteries; and more minefields, trenches and barbed wire protected the draws leading off the beaches. Mortar and artillery positions were then built behind the beaches to shell anyone coming ashore. Where there were open spaces suitable for glider landings or parachute drop zones, Rommel's asparagus (sharpened poles) were designed to kill or maim.

Hitler knew the propaganda value of

holding British territory so the Channel Islands were fortified with some of the most elaborate and extensive defences yet built. Indeed, having fallen to the Nazis in June 1940, they were considered impregnable and the Allies avoided trying to retake them on D-Day for fear of losing too many men and lowering morale with an early defeat. (The garrison on Alderney didn't capitulate until a week after the official Nazi surrender in May 1945.)

The Allies analysed the defences carefully and chose the weaker points where they could come ashore, although they had to balance the strategic value of the landing sites against the likely number of casualties they would sustain.

Chapter 4

Operation Neptune

RIGHT Leonard Dawe was also a gifted footballer

The landings themselves were nearly compromised at the last minute due to an unforeseen problem. It emerged that Leonard Dawe, the headmaster of the Strand School in Effingham, Surrey, had been submitting crosswords to the Daily Telegraph which had many of the code words used during the invasion as answers. Between May 2nd and June 1st 1944 he sent five puzzles to the paper, each of which contained one of the key words: Utah, Omaha, Overlord, Mulberry and Neptune.

Intelligence officers from MI5 arrested him but Dawe persuaded them of his innocence under interrogation. In the months before, his answers had also included the words Gold, Juno and

ABOVE US troops shelter under the bluffs on Omaha Beach

Sword, but he'd often asked children at the school to fill in blank crosswords with unusual words so that he could write cryptic clues for them before submitting them to the paper. As many of the children in the school interacted with the families of servicemen in the area, it seems likely that they had picked up the words before unwittingly passing them on to Dawe. He'd first aroused suspicion when his crossword contained

Dieppe as an answer a couple of days before the disastrous Canadian raid two years earlier, although this seems to have been complete coincidence.

After a day's delay for bad weather, the invasion fleet under the leadership of General Dwight Eisenhower, which was made up of more than 1,000 warships, 4,000 transport ships and landing craft, and another 1,500 ancillary craft and merchant vessels, left ports

across the south coast of England. The fleet boasted 195,000 naval personnel, of whom nearly two thirds were British, one third were American and the minority came from the remaining Allies. There were also 160,000 soldiers scheduled to land on the first day, with approximately half each from Britain and the US and 21,000 Canadians. It was and remains the largest combined operation in military history.

Having broken the German codes and spread disinformation about the attack happening near Calais, the fleet bombarded weaker German positions on five beaches, codenamed Omaha,

ABOVE Sherman tanks are loaded aboard an LCT for the Channel crossing

FAR LEFT A tiny proportion of the convoy crosses the English Channel on the morning of June 6

ABOVE Landing craft approach Utah Beach

Utah, Gold, Juno and Sword. The Atlantic Wall built by German forces occupying Northern France may have been weaker in Normandy but the fighting once the bombardment had stopped and the landing craft had moved onto the beaches was both brutal and bloody. The struggle to secure Omaha Beach was particularly fierce.

Rommel had been recalled from North Africa and had spent a year preparing for the invasion, but the Germans were confident in their existing defences having seen off the raid at Dieppe in 1942. The French Resistance helped provide the Allies with vital information on the beaches – and the pillboxes and bunkers guarding them

ABOVE Canadian forces come ashore on Juno Beach

– and the beaches themselves were carefully chosen for their topography. The Germans could still call on more than a million men and countless Panzers and artillery guns. Rommel was concerned that the Allies might not strike where he anticipated, so he bolstered the defences along nearly 2,000 miles of coastline.

The defenders wrongly believed that the weather was still too bad for amphibious landings and many divisions were stood down. Rommel was even given time off to celebrate his wife's birthday. The British Sixth Airborne Division took advantage of this tactical error and were dropped with Canadian troops behind enemy lines as part of Operation Deadstick.

Chapter 5

Operations Deadstick, Tonga and the Airborne Landings

The airborne assault inland from the beaches was designed to secure the road bridges across the River Orne and the Caen Canal, which would give British forces on Sword Beach an exit to the east. If the paratroopers failed to capture the bridges intact and then hold them against German counterattacks, the 6th Airborne Division would be cut off from the main invasion force, and, if the bridges remained in German hands, they would be able to deploy armoured divisions in a flanking attack to bolster the defences on the beaches. The 6th Airborne's secondary objective was to destroy

ABOVE Pegasus Bridge over the Caen Canal is secured by the Allies on D-Day

FAR LEFT Captain Brian Priday (centre) of the 2nd Airborne Battalion

the German Merville artillery battery, which was within range of Sword Beach and could inflict heavy casualties on the troops coming ashore, and to destroy the bridges over the River Dives.

Major John Howard and Captain Brian Priday took charge of D Company of the 2nd Airborne Battalion, which was tasked with the operation. They trained day and night for weeks with live ammunition in city streets across London and Coventry that had been destroyed by the German bombing campaign. This gave them a feel for the conditions they would encounter in France. Two platoons from B Company

had a maximum payload of seven tons and could carry 30 men or a mixture of men, jeeps, trailers and six-pound field guns.

The Ranville Bridge over the Orne was protected by 50 men from the 736th Grenadiers under Major Hans Schmidt. They were poorly equipped, however, and were mostly Polish and Russian conscripts. The 21st Panzer Division moved in at the end of May to bolster the defence, and Rommel personally oversaw the planting of minefields, wire-braced poles booby-trapped with explosives that were designed to destroy gliders, and the upgrading of the defences around the Merville battery. Although their equipment was also outdated, his 2,000 men had seen action in North Africa and were battle hardened. Two more Panzer divisions were within a few hours of the bridges.

The six gliders were towed into the air by Halifax bombers at RAF Tarrant Rushton. They crossed the Normandy coast just after midnight and three then came down in the defences surrounding the Caen Canal bridge. The landings were heavy and several troops were injured, while one drowned when the remains of the glider slid into a pond.

ABOVE The Bridge over the River Orne

were then added to give support, while 30 men of the Royal Engineers 249th Airborne Field Company under Captain Jock Neilson would carry out demolition or defusing work.

They would travel to their drop zones in six Airspeed Horsa gliders. The Horsa

The Germans may have suspected the invasion to be imminent and they knew the bridges were of vital strategic importance, so it's inexplicable why only a few sentries were on duty when the gliders landed. One was killed immediately while the others managed to alert German machine-gunners with a flare. Number One Platoon threw grenades into bunkers and trenches guarding the bridge, and they then secured the crossing while the engineers checked for explosives underneath.

The German 716th Infantry Division and 21st Panzer Division counterat-tacked at dawn. They would have moved earlier but Panzer formations could only engage the enemy on a direct order from the Führer. Hitler was asleep when the assault began, however, and his staff refused to wake him.

The initial counterattacks were poorly organised and consisted of the odd tank or armoured car with infantry support approaching the bridge. Despite taking heavy casualties, the airborne troops held out until special service commandos of the 6th Airborne Division relieved them. The German counterattacks did intensify during the

ABOVE The three gliders that landed near the Caen Canal bridge

day, however, with the Lufwaffe bombing the bridges and sending coastal craft inland to retake them. The airborne troops and commandos finally received additional help from the 3rd Infantry at 1900 and between them they were able to hold their positions.

The bridge over the Orne was also secured within a few minutes of the gliders landing, although only two of the aircraft made it to the landing site as the pilots of the third mistook the Orne for the River Dives and came down eight miles away. Rather than dwell on the error, the troops secured the bridge over the Dives before heading back to their original objective.

It is a tragedy of war that many of the reinforcements dropped into the area were killed when pathfinders incorrectly marked out the artillery battery at Merville as a target for a squadron of Lancasters and their bombs fell on the 9th Parachute Battalion instead.

The Merville battery may have been a secondary objective but taking it was vital for the safety of the troops coming ashore. It was protected by barbed wire, a minefield, anti-tank ditch, 30 bunkers, an observation post, command post, a flak emplacement, and four casemates containing 150mm artillery pieces. To make matters worse, many of the airborne troops were dropped in the wrong place due to navigational errors and thick cloud cover and, when the battalions of the 3rd and 5th Parachute Brigades finally reached the gun battery, they were below half strength.

Colonel Terence Otway had orders to take the battery by 0530 so that it was in their hands by the time the bombardment before the beach assault began. That left him little choice but to attack with only 150 men, although they were then joined by survivors of the pathfinder group. Otway divided them into four assault groups (one for each casemate) and they moved in at 0430. Although they took heavy casualties, they secured the gun emplacements by lobbing grenades into the air vents.

BELOW German troops examine a Waco glider

They then disabled the howitzers inside (one was later put back into action when the Germans retook the site) before ousting a German platoon from the village of Le Plein. Otway was then forced to abandon his remaining objectives because he'd lost more than half of his men.

The 6th Airborne Division was a much larger force consisting of 239 support aircraft and 89 gliders, the latter of which began landing in the minutes after 0330. They set up a command post but later moved their headquarters to Ranville, from where they linked up with the 3rd and 5th Parachute Brigades as well as the Special Service Brigade. A further 220 Horsa and Hamilcar gliders landed late on June 6th to complete the airborne invasion. By midnight, the entire 6th Airborne had taken up positions protecting the eastern flank of the seaborne invasion, and by 12th June they'd achieved all of their goals. Of the 8,500 men who landed in the first two days, only 800 were lost. By the end of August the division had advanced to the mouth of the Seine but it was then withdrawn from the frontline.

The American 82nd and 101st Airborne in the west weren't as fortunate, although Lieutenant-General Omar Bradley's plan was well-conceived: land two airborne divisions on the Cherbourg Peninsula to seize the beach causeways (101st) and block the east and west corridors from German reinforcements (82nd). The initial plan was to use gliders to deliver most of the men and machinery but several training accidents forced them to revert to a parachute airdrop at night. A smaller number of gliders would then follow throughout the next day.

By now Rommel knew an invasion was coming so the defences in the peninsula were beefed up. The American drop zones had to be moved accordingly, and the pathfinders landed early on the morning of June 6th to set up beacons and marker lights. Due to navigational errors, cloud cover, anti-aircraft fire and the proximity of German forces, only two of the drop zones were able to show their landing lights.

Several hundred C-47s then dropped six parachute infantry regiments of nearly 2,000 men each into the war zone. Despite the formation over the Channel and initial run to the drop zones going smoothly, many aircraft

came in too low and hundreds of paratroopers were injured when their parachutes didn't fully open in time. Many more were killed by tracer fire on the way down. The main problem, however, was the fact that the drop took place at night because it left troops scattered across the countryside trying to home in on beacons that weren't

ABOVE The Merville artillery position was heavily bombed before the 6th Airborne moved in to capture the emplacements

FAR LEFT A Panzer of the 21st Division

ABOVE Lieutenant-General Omar Bradley (left) listens as Major-General Joseph Collins describes how Cherbourg was taken

of landing men near their drop zones. The 3rd Battalion only came up against token resistance and managed to secure the town of Sainte-Mère-Église by 0430, but the 1st Battalion became bogged down and couldn't capture two bridges over the River Merderet until several days later.

Reinforcements for both the 101st and 82nd came in on 52 gliders loaded with anti-tank weapons and troops just before dawn. Almost all of the 101st landed within two miles of their targets, but a third of the 82nd missed theirs after entering the same troublesome cloud that had hindered the parachute drop. Despite the missed landing, the gliders brought much-needed support to the paratroopers, a situation that was further boosted when another 208 gliders in two more waves (under fighter escort) overflew the beaches and landed four battalions of artillery.

The glider missions continued the following morning, most of which were successful, although several of the 82nd came down under intense fire from the retreating Germans. Two supply parachute drops later on June 7th also took heavy casualties, with 14 C-47s lost. By this time only 2,500 men of the 6,928

functioning properly.

Although the first wave did achieve a number of objectives, the drop was disorganised and it took hours before they were a cohesive unit. The second wave, meanwhile, began an hour later and enjoyed much greater success in terms

ABOVE Men of the 101st Airborne with a captured Swastika on June 8th

troops in the 101st Airborne were in position for the advance inland (so more than 4,000 weren't yet under the control of their divisional headquarters).

The 82nd were in better shape as they had regrouped around the village of Sainte-Mère-Église but there were isolated pockets of paratroopers west of the River Merderet who had to hold out against the Germans for up to five days. By June 9th they were still struggling to control the bridge across the Merderet but they did eventually force their way over to link up with the pockets of paratroopers behind enemy lines. By June 19th they'd secured the villages of Chef-du-Pont, Montebourg, Baupte, Pont l'Abbé and Saint-Sauveur-le-Vicomte. On July 3rd the 82nd made its final advance towards La Haye-du-Puits before being incorporated into the 90th Infantry.

On June 13th the German 17th SS Panzergrenadiers and 37th SS Regiment attacked the 101st and pushed them back past Carentan until the 2nd Armored Division arrived to repel them. Two days later, the 101st was also integrated into the US VIII Corps and sent back to England to recover.

Casualties on both sides during the American airborne assault were considerable. Almost all of the 222 Horsa gliders were destroyed on landing or shortly afterwards by German ground troops. Although most of the 295 Waco gliders survived the landings, they were usually abandoned in the fields where they came down. On D-Day itself, both the 82nd and 101st lost more than 1,200 men, which rose to approximately 4,500 from each by the end of the month (more two-thirds of those who parachuted in). Germany lost 21,000 men defending the Cherbourg Peninsula.

The high rate of attrition was blamed on the pilots of the troop transports missing their drop zones, but the more experienced paratroopers were used to missed landings and having men scattered over wide areas, as were most of the British along the coast. Bad weather, poor visibility, heavy German resistance, poor radio communication, the inexperience of the pathfinders setting up the beacons, and a host of other factors combined to make the operation more difficult. However, the confusion among Allied personnel came with a blessing because German defences were split (and therefore weakened) by the men landing all around their positions.

Chapter 6

Utah

Utah Beach was only considered as a landing option towards the end of the planning phase for D-Day. There weren't initially enough landing craft available but when more were supplied to the invasion fleet, the three-mile beach between Pouppeville and La Madeleine was chosen as the right (western) flank. Along with Omaha Beach to the east, it would be assaulted by predominantly American troops.

At four o'clock in the morning, a small contingent of marines swam ashore to secure a German observation post, but it was unoccupied. The second phase of the attack involved 20 Higgins Boat (a small wooden amphibious landing craft carrying around 40 men) of the 8th Infantry and eight tank landing craft. A second wave of 32 Higgins Boats with additional troops, engineers and demolition teams followed. Two

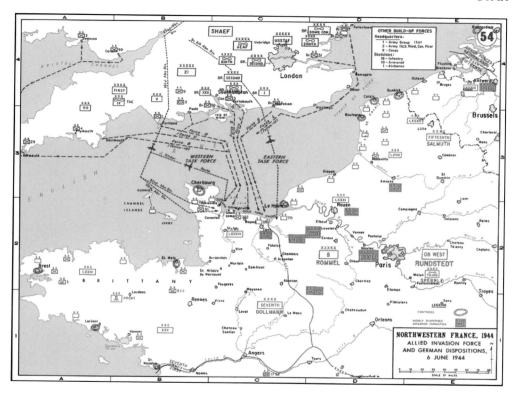

NORTHWESTERN FRANCE, 1944
ALLIED INVASION FORCE
AND GERMAN DISPOSITIONS,
6 JUNE 1944

more waves were scheduled to land more tanks and combat engineers shortly afterwards.

In all, around 24,000 men of the VII Corps, 4th Infantry and 90th Infantry were supported by the 101st Airborne Division, which parachuted in around Vierville, and the 82nd Airborne, which dropped in to Sainte-Mère-Église to protect the right flank. At H-Hour (the

ABOVE A map of the Allied invasion on the Normandy beaches

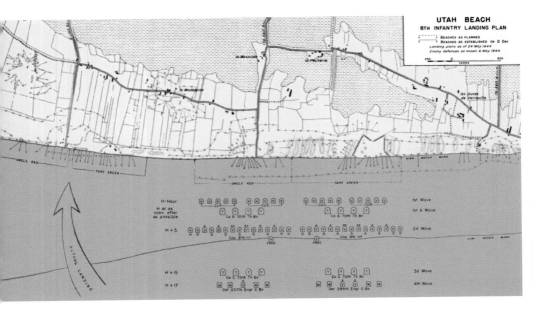

ABOVE The landing plan for the 8th Infantry on Utah Beach

designated time for the main assault), the landings began and 600 men waded unopposed onto Utah Beach. They were slightly south of their intended position but there was no confusion as resistance was so light.

The situation was further eased by the presence of General Theodore Roosevelt Jr (President Roosevelt's son) who was assistant commander of the 4th Infantry. He risked his life by making a personal reconnaissance of the beachhead to make sure they could still reach their rendezvous points for the push inland. He then guided two more battalions into the beach and advised each regiment on their new objectives. He was later awarded the Medal of Honor for his bravery. Here is the citation:

For gallantry and intrepidity at the risk of his life above and beyond the call of duty on 6th June 1944 in France. After two verbal requests to accompany the leading assault elements in the Normandy invasion had been denied, Brig. Gen. Roosevelt's written request for this mission was approved and he landed with the first wave of forces assaulting the enemy-held beaches. He repeatedly led groups from the beach, over the seawall and established them inland. His valor, courage, and presence in the very front of the attack and his complete unconcern at being under heavy fire inspired the troops to heights of enthusiasm and self-sacrifice. Although the enemy had the beach under constant direct fire, Brig. Gen. Roosevelt moved from one locality to another, rallying men around him and personally leading them against the enemy. Under his seasoned, precise, calm, and unfaltering leadership, assault troops reduced beach strong-points and rapidly moved inland with minimum casualties. He thus contributed substantially to the successful establishment of the beachhead in France.

ABOVE Allied forces landing on Utah Beach

Twenty minutes later, Captain Pike's Royal Marine Commandos joined American forces on the beach. Only now did the German defences try to protect the beachhead but their 709th and 352nd Infantry had been split by the airborne paratroopers landing at their rear and clearing them from the beach exits. They'd been further weakened by the intense naval bombardment prior to the landings, and the fortifications this far west weren't as formidable.

Utah Beach was therefore the main success story in the initial phase of the landing operation: the bunkers behind the beach were destroyed by bombers beforehand; most of the tanks made it ashore because the water was shallow and they were deployed close to the beach; although many of the landings were to the south of their intended positions, the beach exits were still

available; only 200 lives were lost; and by the end of the day, 20,000 men of the 4th Infantry had linked up with the parachute regiments of the 101st Airborne and they advanced swiftly inland against light German resistance that couldn't organise a counterattack.

How those landing at Omaha Beach would have hoped for a similar reception…

ABOVE A Higgins Boat disgorges troops onto the beach

LEFT Theodore Roosevelt in Northern France

Chapter 7

Omaha

Although the Royal Navy provided some of the naval bombardment on Omaha Beach, US warships delivered most of the ordnance and the troops on the ground were exclusively American. The primary objective of the landing was to secure the beach, push five miles inland and link British forces on Gold Beach to the east with the American infantry divisions moving inland from Utah Beach to the west. If they could form a continuous frontline by the end of the day, a German counterattack would be less likely and/or less effective.

The naval bombardment has been criticised for being inadequate, however. Only one battleship, two cruisers and six destroyers were deployed, which was far less support than the landings on the Pacific Islands received. General Omar Bradley motivated the troops with a rousing speech about how the German positions would be blasted to pieces before they went ashore, but this never happened. Indeed Rear Admiral John Hall branded the lack of support criminal and suggested that casualties on the beach were so high because the bombardment was too light.

The beach itself was around five miles long from Sainte-Honorine-des-Pertes to Vierville-sur-Mer, and it was known to be heavily defended by the German 716th and 352nd Infantry Divisions, although the latter was believed to be stationed at Saint-Lô 20 miles inland so the Allies were confident of securing the beach. Rommel, however, had

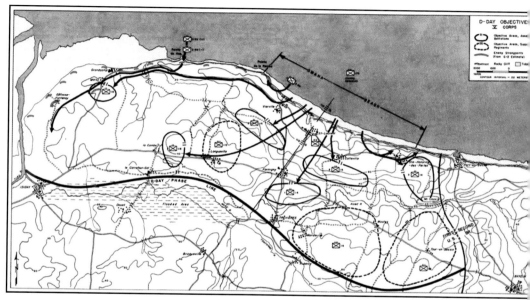

ABOVE The Allied map showing American D-Day objectives on Omaha Beach

ordered the 352nd along with two extra battalions to the waterfront with support from the artillery of the 1st and 4th battalions. This oversight proved to be the second Allied failing during the landing on Omaha Beach (after the light bombardment) as it exposed American forces to 7,800 infantrymen, eight artillery bunkers, 35 pillboxes, 18 anti-tank guns, 45 rocket launcher sites and 85 machinegun nests.

The American 29th Infantry and nine companies of Army Rangers took the western end of the beach while the battle-hardened 1st Infantry took the east. The beach itself sloped gently up to a shingle bank on the high-tide line. Beyond this was a sandy embankment at the foot of steep rocky escarpments around 40 metres (135 feet) high.

OMAHA

There were several breaks in the bluffs – known as draws – but they were all well defended.

In fact the Atlantic Wall was designed solely to stop an invasion force on the beach as the defences did not extend more than a mile or so inland. German forces had built four lines of heavy steel anti-tank defences (known as Belgian Gates) with mines secured to the uprights, behind which was a line of wooden tree trunks driven into the beach and capped with anti-tank mines. The third line of defence was a row of ramps that were designed to flip the landing craft before blowing them up with explosives. And the fourth tier was a line of hedgehogs (crossed steel

ABOVE General Omar Bradley surveys proceedings on Omaha from the bridge of the USS Augusta. The other men (from left to right) are Rear Admiral Alan Kirk, Bradley, Rear Admiral Arthur Struble and Major-General Hugh Keen

girders) that were also mined. Still more mines were scattered along the bluffs and in the exits from the beach.

On top of the escarpment, German defenders were housed in reinforced pillboxes and around 15 casemates, of which the largest eight held heavy artillery pieces. The strongholds were linked by trenches and tunnels and protected by minefields and barbed wire. No part of the beach was undefended so casualties on both sides were expected to be high.

Half an hour before the landing craft were deployed, Allied aircraft and ships bombarded the coastal defences. Then the tanks and infantry advanced to the beach, with the aim being to clear

OMAHA

the escarpment after two hours and allow their vehicles and other hardware off the beach an hour later. The Allies boasted overwhelming superiority – 34,000 men, 3,300 vehicles, 200 landing craft of varying size and cargo, and naval support from 122 surface ships – but the assault ran into trouble immediately.

At least 10 landing craft sank before they reached the beach because the weather was still poor. Many more were kept afloat by severely seasick soldiers using their helmets to bail water from the bilges. Smoke from the bombardment lingered and obscured the landing sites so many of the craft missed the landmarks designating their disembar-

kation points. Still more ran down soldiers trying to escape the sinking craft or collided with tanks that had been stranded in water that was too deep.

As the bedraggled force stormed the beach, they came under intense fire from the German defences. The naval bombardment may have had some effect on the casemates, pillboxes and machinegun nests, but the bombers had dropped their ordnance too far inland as they were afraid of damaging the landing craft. This meant that the German defences were largely intact, and their artillery soon wiped out half of the 743rd Tank Battalion and another three DD (amphibious) tanks from A Company.

The infantry landings were similarly compromised: only two of the nine companies came ashore where they were supposed to, and one drifted so far east they didn't land for another 90 minutes. Sandbars raised by the poor weather beached some of the landing craft more than 100 metres (330 feet) from the shore so the men had to struggle through chest-deep water with heavy packs and assault weapons while under withering enemy fire.

When they finally reached the beach,

they were exhausted, and clambering up the shingle incline only slowed them further. Hundreds were killed by mortars and small-arms fire as they crossed the 200 metres (660 feet) of open ground beneath the bluffs. Amidst all the noise and smoke, and with many of their officers killed before reaching the shingle bank, communication between companies became impossible and the initial thrust lost its impetus.

No more so was this evident on the flanks: in the east at Fox Green and Easy Red beaches (the main beaches were all subdivided into smaller sections), the companies lost half their men, while those at Dog Green Beach in the west had been decimated. The Rangers

ABOVE Men wade into battle under heavy fire from the bluffs

alongside had also been whittled down by half, with many being forced to take cover behind the German obstacles on the beach. (It is testament to Steven Spielberg's talent as a filmmaker that the horrific opening scenes of Saving Private Ryan, which depict the Army Rangers landing at Omaha Beach, were universally praised for their accuracy.)

With the infantry in total disarray and unable to accomplish any of their immediate objectives, the next wave of engineers landed. They too had been pushed off course by a combination of the weather and their inability to pick out landmarks, and only five landing craft arrived at their designated zone.

Three came ashore so far off course that there was no infantry or armour to protect them, while the rest had to improvise routes through the obstacles. Although these obstacles needed to be cleared by explosives, most were now providing cover for the infantry pinned down on the beach so the engineers were largely redundant. Nevertheless, they eventually managed to clear six routes at Dog White, Easy Green and Easy Red, which was better than expected given that they'd lost 40% of their men.

The second phase of the Omaha landings was much larger but it suffered from the same problems. Also,

ABOVE Wounded
servicemen are helped
ashore after their
landing craft was
destroyed

the infantry that was ashore and supposed to be providing cover for the second phase was in such disarray that casualties were nearly as high as during the initial assault. Only the troops from Group C of the 116th Regimental Combat Team (RCT) were relatively unscathed as they missed their landing and were now alone at Dog White to the east of the main beach. They became a focal point for many disbanded companies and rangers and they continued to shelter in the lee of the bluffs under cover of the smoke from grass fires on the top of the escarpment. Group F, meanwhile, were also doing better than expected and a 50-man patrol mounted a half-hearted assault on the bluffs to

BELOW Assault troops shelter under the bluffs

the east of the Les Moulins defences. It was too weak to penetrate the German strongholds, however, and they were forced back down to the beach.

Fox Green was the easternmost part of Omaha Beach and it also became a gathering point for those separated from their companies. Two more companies of the 3rd Battalion joined them when they missed their landing. Although men and supplies continued to pour ashore throughout the day, many half-tracks and jeeps were lost in the surf and many more became bogged down in the obstacles on the beach. More than 2,500 American men lost

their lives in the opening exchanges and many of those who survived now found themselves in combat for the first time. Maintaining morale in the face of such adversity became the biggest problem, and, as many companies were now leaderless and injured men were drowning on the incoming tide, the situation deteriorated further.

German reports of the battle for Omaha Beach varied wildly. An hour after the first wave had landed, the commander of the 726th Grenadier Battalion reported that 200 American troops had advanced beyond Fox Green Beach, breached the bluffs and were attacking the defenders from the rear. With the situation deteriorating for the Germans at Gold Beach, reinforcements were sent there instead, leaving the casemates on Omaha poorly defended in the face of persistent American attacks.

However, these reports conflict with

ABOVE Omaha Beach on the afternoon of D-Day

the 352nd Division's belief that at 1330, seven hours after the first men came ashore, all US troops were still pinned on the beach. The waves of reinforcements were apparently bogged down behind the obstacles at the tide line and at least 10 tanks were on fire. The truth lies somewhere between: most American soldiers were still trapped on the beach, but some were making forays inland through the draws (natural breaks in the land to the rear of the beaches) and along the bluffs.

Artillery support from the ships in the Channel was now essential to eliminate the threat from the German positions on the escarpment. However, after the Operation Tiger disaster there was a fear of hitting their own troops so the ships concentrated their fire on the flanks as visibility on the main beach was still poor. The smaller destroyers were able to approach within 1,000 metres (3,300 feet) of the beach and, although several almost ran aground, the USS McCook destroyed one of the 75mm emplacements on the bluff and the USS Frankford took their fire control from a stranded tank on the beach that was still blasting away at German positions.

Despite being scattered along the beach, American forces began to coalesce in pockets beneath the bluffs and around the draws leading inland. The 2nd Rangers at Dog Green soon scaled the cliffs by the Vierville draw, while Group B of the 116th RCT eventually disabled the artillery position defending the beach exit. Group C and the 5th Rangers pushed inland from Dog White and established positions along the bluff by taking another artillery position.

The 3rd Battalion of the 116th assaulted the artillery position defending the draw at Les Moulins and had reached the top of the bluff by 0900. Five minutes later, German defenders reported losing two more artillery

positions. Men from G Company then moved south into Colleville to take the German command post.

In a remarkable show of bravery, and in a move that would make a difference to those soon to land on the beach in another wave, Captain Bob Sheppard and Lieutenant John Spalding recruited two men for an assault on the formidable WN-64 casemate (the Allies had labelled all the German positions with codenames). Between them, the four men engaged the enemy in and around the artillery position for two hours. They then managed to negotiate the

BELOW USS Frankford provided support to the Omaha landings

Colonel George Taylor

surrender of 21 German soldiers just as they were about to fire upon Colonel George Taylor's men of the 16th RCT who were coming ashore.

Taylor was so concerned about the carnage on the beach that he uttered one of the most famous lines from the conflict: "Two kinds of people are staying on this beach: the dead and those about to die. Let's get the hell out of here!" He assigned men to any available NCO (non-commissioned officer) and instructed them to head south through the breach forged by G Company.

At the eastern end of the beach, more men had come ashore under lighter resistance, and they soon knocked out another of the heavy gun emplacements. If these troops were to achieve their objectives, the key element now was leadership. So many companies had been separated that the groups of men who were advancing inland all had different goals. Men like Taylor reassigned them so that the force that secured the artillery positions and set up command posts had a better idea of what they were supposed to be doing.

Despite some companies moving inland, however, not all of the draws had been secured and several German artillery positions were still operating. The engineers hadn't managed to clear the obstacles on the beach either, so the following waves of men and machinery were forced to come ashore at Easy Green and Easy Red. The battle appeared to be swinging further in the Germans' favour when landings were suspended because of the concentration of enemy fire on the two openings through the obstacles. As the weather was still quite poor, the backlog of vehicles became jammed just off the beach and many were lost. Indeed of the 13 DUKWs (amphibious trucks) used by the 111th Field Artillery, only one managed to offload its howitzer. The rest were either swamped, became lost or were destroyed as they approached the beach.

Taylor then directed the tanks to try to force an exit at the Colleville draw but only three made it to the rallying point and two were immediately destroyed by enemy fire from the bluffs. Reinforcements were still stranded in the congestion offshore so it took until 1130 to take the final gun emplacement guarding the draw. Troop movements inland were still hampered by mines and small-arms fire from the retreating

LEFT General Dietrich Kraiss

ABOVE More supplies and men pour ashore in the days after the initial landing on Omaha

Germans but by 1300 the navy had finally silenced the casemate protecting the Vierville draw. However, German resistance prevented the exit being fully operational until later that night.

As the routes off the beach slowly opened to traffic, the congestion offshore and on the beach itself began to ease. With the tide retreating, the engineers who'd been largely ineffective

were now able to clear more openings in the obstacles and traffic was soon flooding ashore through 13 breaches.

A battalion of German reinforcements and an anti-tank company from the 915th Regiment were then dispatched from Gold Beach to the east to help repel the Americans on Omaha. The two sides met at Colleville at 1430 but, having established a foothold on

ABOVE Omaha Beach

the beach and command posts inland, the Americans were in a much better position than they had been an hour earlier and they contributed to heavy German losses. German reserves from the 352nd Division were more concerned with the British on Gold Beach so they were held back. This proved to be a serious tactical error because the units defending Brittany, which were dispatched to Omaha, took too long to mobilise. Once they were underway, they were targeted by Allied aircraft now enjoying air superiority and they also suffered heavy losses.

General Dietrich Kraiss realised that German forces defending the beach had all but been eliminated so he ordered the remains of the 352nd to surround the Americans and prevent them breaking out of Colleville. The defence of the beach had been organised into a single line of resistance and there were far fewer pillboxes and machinegun nests inland. Indeed the German retreat was characterised by staunch defence where possible but mainly guerrilla-style raiding tactics by small numbers of men. One machinegun nest, for example, managed to contain the entire 5th Ranger Battalion. When platoons attempted to circle the nest, they ran into a second nest, and the next platoon ran into a third and so on. It was this staggered defence, with each nest providing covering fire for two more, which halted the American advance for another four hours.

By nine o'clock in the evening, the final infantrymen and supplies came ashore, but it had been a costly day in terms of men and equipment lost. Only 5% of the supplies made it ashore, while 50 tanks, 50 landing craft and 26 heavy guns were also lost. Another 500 men also died during the second and third waves. Such was the confusion in the first two hours after the initial landing that the Commander of the First Army, Lieutenant-General Omar Bradley, was on the verge of evacuating the beach. Montgomery was equally concerned and almost ordered a retreat so the surviving infantry

BELOW The gravestone of Lieutenant-General Lesley McNair in the American cemetery overlooking Omaha Beach

LESLEY J. MC NAIR
LT GEN ARMY GROUND FORCES
MINNESOTA JULY 25 1944

could be diverted to Gold Beach.

The Allied objectives on Omaha Beach weren't achieved until two days later, partly due to the pockets of German resistance behind the American front line and partly due to continued shelling from artillery positions inland. Supplies were still finding it difficult to get through the abandoned and destroyed vehicles on the beach, while the 16th Infantry was still fighting the German 916th and 726th Grenadiers in the WN-63 casemate.

With Colleville now secure, the infantry moved on to Formigny, but the town didn't fall into American hands until June 8th. The following morning, American forces pushed east to link up with the British XXX Corps from Gold. The 116th Infantry and 2nd Rangers then mopped up the last of the defenders on the bluffs. When the 3rd Regiment of the 29th Division took the town of Isigny, they established contact with the 101st Airborne, which meant that Omaha was now also linked with Utah.

Over the next few days the German 352nd and 726th were rendered ineffective and the beachhead was deemed secure, and by June 16th the first Mulberry harbour was operational inside a breakwater of scuttled ships that were no longer needed. The LSTs were now able to unload vast quantities of supplies at the harbour – 11,000 troops, 2,000 vehicles and 9,000 tons of equipment – but a tremendous storm raged from June 19th to June 22nd and completely destroyed Mulberry A. It was too costly in terms of time and resources to repair it so supplies were landed directly on the beach from then on. In the next three months, 1,500,000 tons of equipment and 600,000 men came ashore on Omaha Beach and nearly 100,000 casualties were evacuated.

Geographically, the beach remains much the same today and many of the coastal defences can be visited. The American cemetery at the top of the bluff just outside Colleville contains the remains of 9,387 servicemen, most of whom were killed during the initial invasion. It also has the graves of Medal of Honor recipient Theodore Roosevelt Jr, who died of a heart attack a month after the invasion (just before he was going to be promoted to Major-General and take command of the 90th Infantry), and General Lesley McNair, the joint highest-ranking American officer to be killed in action during the war.

Chapter 8

Gold

The British 50th Infantry Division was assigned to the beach between Arromanches and Ver-sur-Mer, with its secondary initiative being to push inland to Bayeux and sever the German supply lines into Caen. The beach also needed to be secured so that a second Mulberry harbour could be built.

The first two infantry brigades were to establish the beachhead, while the second wave pushed south with tank support from the 8th Armoured Brigade. In the west, 47 Commando would capture Port-en-Bessin and before linking up with American forces on Omaha Beach.

The German 716th Static and 916th Infantry Grenadiers were assigned to the east and west respectively, while several artillery batteries around the villages inland, notably Mont-Fleury, Creully and Crepon, covered the beach. Half a mile further inland, four 155mm howitzers were based on the cliffs at Longues-sur-Mer. The 441st Battalion of Russian conscripts defended the centre of the beach with 50mm guns housed in small concrete bunkers and 75mm weapons in pillboxes.

The British initiated the action by bombing German defences along the cliffs. HMS Ajax then moved in with three more cruisers, the battleship Warspite and the French cruiser Georges Leygues. The command ship, HMS Bulolo took heavy fire from the battery at Longues-sur-Mer and was forced to retreat but Commodore Sir Cyril Douglas-Pennant insisted she

remained on station for the duration of the beach assault.

With the German defences softened up by the bombardment, two assault brigades moved towards the beach at King Sector. At 0730 (an hour later than the Americans on Omaha because of the tidal surge) the first wave of troops landed but they were immediately bogged down by the marshy conditions and raking German machinegun fire. The beach was also littered with anti-tank obstacles and mines, which had to be defused by the engineers.

A higher tide than expected con-cealed many of the obstacles and mines, which meant they weren't cleared in the initial thrust. The decision was taken, therefore, to ride over the mines in the landing craft and ram them onto the beach. The amphibious tanks were also landed directly on the beach, but they came under intense fire and lost their commanding officer immediately. The decision was vindicated, however, as there was no German armour protect-ing the coast and the tanks with infan-try support quickly overcame German resistance. Just before 0830, battalions from the Royal Marines landed to give

ABOVE Commandos of the British 50th Infantry come ashore on Gold Beach

ABOVE The remains of the Longues-sur-Mer artillery position

FAR RIGHT More German defences guarding Gold Beach

support and three beach exits were cleared shortly afterwards.

German defences in Jig Sector were weak and the 6th Green Howards came ashore with the amphibious tanks of the Westminster Dragoons. Having secured the landing zone, the Howards advanced inland to take the artillery batteries. It was during this engagement that the only Victoria Cross on D-Day was earned.

As the Green Howards moved inland, Company Sergeant Major Stanley Hollis realised that two German pillboxes near the Mont Fleury gun battery had been missed. Hollis charged the first position, shooting two defenders dead and capturing another five after clearing the position with a grenade.

He then singlehandedly attacked the second pillbox, taking another 26 men prisoner, before clearing a connecting trench. A short while later, he led an attack on a machinegun position. In the aftermath, he was told that two of his men had been trapped in a house. He deliberately drew enemy fire to give them time to escape, and then attacked and neutralised the German position.

Hollis was injured later in the campaign and returned to England. He was decorated with the Victoria Cross – the highest award for gallantry for any member of British or Commonwealth forces – by King George VI on October 10th 1944. The citation explained his heroism on the day:

While in Normandy on 6th June 1944, Company Sergeant-Major Stanley Hollis went with his company commander to investigate two German pillboxes, which had been bypassed as the company moved inland from the beaches. Hollis instantly rushed straight at the first pillbox, firing his Sten gun. He then jumped on top of the pillbox, recharged his magazine, threw a grenade in through the door and fired his Sten gun into it, killing two Germans and taking the remainder prisoner. Later the same day, C.S.M. Hollis pushed right forward to engage an enemy field gun with a PIAT [antitank weapon] from a house at 50 yards range. He later learned that two of his men had stayed behind in the house. In full view of the enemy, who were continually firing at him, he went forward alone and distracted their attention from the other men. Under cover of his diversion, the two men were able to get back. Wherever the fighting was heaviest he appeared, displaying the utmost gallantry. It was largely due through his heroism and resourcefulness that his company's objectives were achieved and casualties were not heavier. He saved the lives of many of his men.

GOLD

The last commando unit came ashore in Item Sector, which was to the east of the beach. They immediately pushed inland towards the port of Bessin, which needed to be taken to allow the PLUTO oil and supplies ashore. The staunch German defence of the port kept the British out for another two days but it finally fell on June 8th.

German forces of the 352nd Reserves were in position to launch a counter-strike on Gold Beach on the morning of June 6th but paratroopers from the US 101st Airborne had landed near the Vire estuary and they were diverted there instead. By the time they'd returned to within striking distance of Gold Beach,

British forces had established the beach-head and, after a token assault had been repelled, the opportunity was lost.

By midnight, 25,000 men of the British 2nd Army under Lieutenant-General Miles Dempsey had landed at Gold Beach. Only 400 men were lost on the first day, and the Northumbrian Infantry had already made it to the outskirts of Bayeux. As Arromanches had fallen at 2100, the British now had a beachhead six miles wide and six miles deep. Although they'd linked with Canadian forces on Juno Beach, they had not yet joined American forces because the fighting at Omaha had been so heavy. British forces then launched

Operation Perch to drive further inland and secure Caen, while the second Mulberry harbour was being built in Item Sector.

On June 9th, however, Caen was still held by the retreating Germans. Montgomery, Dempsey and Bradley met to discuss the 2nd Army taking the city in a pincer movement under the codename Operation Wild Oats. The 51st Highland Infantry and the 4th Armoured Brigade crossed the Orne via the bridgehead secured by the 6th Airborne, while the western arm of the pincer would consist of the XXX Corps. To add extra weight to the attack, Montgomery suggested landing men of the 1st Airborne between the pincers but Sir Trafford Leigh-Mallory refused to allow a parachute or glider incursion as the area was still in German hands.

Indeed the elite German 21st Panzer Division and the fanatical Hitler Youth under Field Marshal Gerd von Rundstedt immediately mobilised from their positions in the south to counter the threat. However, Allied air superiority meant the tanks, mobile artillery and other vehicles were vulnerable and they lost more than 200 on the 90-mile journey to intercept British and American

forces. They did manage to link up with the remains of the 716th Static Infantry, however, which then moved into positions on the outskirts of the city.

Early on June 9th, XXX Corps forged a link with American soldiers from Omaha, and then the 50th Infantry came up against Panzer Lehr units in the outskirts of Tilly-sur-Seulles. The Panzers, along with more tanks from

ABOVE C.S.M Stanley Hollis was awarded the only Victoria Cross on D-Day

BELOW LEFT A British Centaur tank heads south during Operation Perch

BELOW RIGHT Tanks from the 7th Armoured Division roll inland from Gold Beach on D-Day

the 12th SS counterattacked but it was eventually repelled the following morning. By June 11th Allied forces had taken the town centre but more counterattacks from tanks of the Panzer Lehr forced them to withdraw. Hitler was so encouraged by these small gains that he ordered Rommel to push the Allies all

the way back to the beach. Both sides suffered severe casualties in the following days as ferocious defence from the 6th Airborne protecting the vital bridges countered determined German advances.

Montgomery was eventually forced to rethink the pincer attack because

his flanks were too weak. He decided instead on a powerful frontal assault from the entire 50th Division with support from the RAF and artillery from the 7th Armoured Division. Although the Allies did advance into the villages surrounding Caen, German resistance was fierce and casualties on both sides were high. In fact the fighting between the XXX Corps and the Panzer Lehr was so intense in Tilly-sur-Seulles that the village was completely obliterated.

By the end of June the Panzer Lehr Division had lost 3,000 men and 430 tanks, halftracks and artillery pieces.

The 12th SS Panzers had lost a further 1,500 men and 41 tanks, while the 21st Panzers lost 2,000 men and 30 tanks. The British suffered equally heavy casualties, losing around 5,500 men and 40 tanks. The engagement was so costly that Montgomery had to concede that Caen could not be taken in a direct strike or by surrounding it. Instead, RAF Bomber Command levelled the city and finally forced the Germans out in late July. It had been an extremely brutal engagement that resulted in countless civilian deaths, 51,000 Allied soldiers lost and an unknown number of Germans.

ABOVE A stranded Tiger tank

Chapter 9

Juno

Juno Beach ran from Courseulles-sur-Mer in the west (next to Gold Beach) to Saint-Aubin-sur-Mer (just west of Sword). The aim of the landing force was to provide assistance to the British flanks as well as capturing an airfield at Carpiquet. The beach was shallow and it was only around 100 metres (330 feet) from the shoreline to the seawall. It also led directly into the villages as there were no bluffs or cliffs.

Canadian forces of the 3rd Infantry at Juno were backed by Royal Marine Commandos but they faced stern opposition in the shape of two heavy and nine medium batteries along with countless machinegun nests and pill-boxes manned by the German 716th Infantry, the 21st Panzers and the 12th Panzer Division of the Hitler Youth.

Rommel had personally inspected the Atlantic Wall defences along the Normandy coast in the months before the invasion and Juno was particularly well defended. There were rows of obstacles just above the low-tide mark, while machinegun positions and forti-fied bunkers lined the beach exits. There were also mortar platoons, minefields and extra fortifications around the harbour at Courseulles. In all, the defences were manned by 8,000 infantrymen.

RAF Bomber Command, which included 230 Canadian aircraft, tar-geted the coastal defences from 2330 on June 5th until 0515 on D-Day itself. By then, they'd flown more than 1,000 sorties and dropped more than 5,000 tons of ordnance on German positions, the largest single bombing campaign of the war to date. However, poor visibility and minor navigational errors (also a feature of the glider incursions) meant that the defences at Omaha, Gold and Juno were virtually intact.

The naval bombardment at Juno was launched by HMS Belfast at 0530,

and the German battery at Longues was soon silenced by HMS Ajax. HMS Diadem then destroyed the battery at Beny-sur-Mer. Forty minutes later, navy destroyers moved towards the beach and began a saturation bombardment against smaller installations. Even the landing craft had been equipped with field guns, and they were sup-

BELOW Erwin Rommel inspects the Atlantic Wall defences

ABOVE The American
air force bombs Pointe
du Hoc in the build-up
to the invasion

plemented by yet more bombing from RAF fighter-bombers and Typhoons of the USAF.

The bombardment is generally considered to have had little effect on the German positions. Bomber Command's efforts were largely thwarted by cloud cover, which meant they missed most of the bigger batteries, and those that were hit were so well protected that damage was light. The naval engagement was also inaccurate due to the rising seas and it wasn't heavy enough to destroy the reinforced concrete bunkers, but it did force the German defenders to take cover and must have sapped their morale.

Indeed the bombardment was so intense that the landings had to be delayed by a few minutes. This meant the Canadians hit the beach at high tide in the middle of another row of obstacles laid by the Germans. They then had to disembark the landing craft under fire and casualties were high. Despite coming ashore with heavy armour themselves, they lost half their men from the first wave because they were targeted by three casemates and 12 machinegun positions.

As with the other main beaches, Juno was divided up into sectors. The 7th Canadian Infantry with assault companies of the Royal Winnipeg Rifles, the Canadian Scottish Regiment and a squadron of the 1st Hussars landed at Mike Red and Mike Green, while the Regina Rifles and a second squadron of the Hussars landed on Nan Red and Nan Green. As German resistance varied from barbed wire with the odd machinegun nest to heavy artillery, casualties varied from light to extremely heavy as they cleared the beach and moved inland. Whereas to the west the naval bombardment had accounted for the main 75mm gun emplacement, to the east the Regina Rifles encountered

The cruiser HMS Belfast joins the bombardment of German positions on Juno

ABOVE Canadian soldiers secure the beach

FAR RIGHT Men of the Royal Winnipeg rifles approach the beach

an 88mm position with metre-thick walls that was protected by heavy machineguns.

The amphibious tanks from B Squadron managed to silence another 75mm emplacement at Courseulles, while the 88mm position was also eventually taken. As soon as the guns had fallen silent, two reserve companies came ashore and pushed into the villages of Banville and Sainte-Croix-sur-Mer. A Company and the 1st Hussars cleared enemy positions quickly, while C and D Companies stormed Courseulles and eventually claimed the village. The second wave of the Scottish Regiment, however, remained pinned down on the beach for another hour.

At Nan White, the Queen's Own Rifles of Canada ran into desperate German defence outside the village of Bernières, while B Company missed its landing point on the beach by 200 metres (660 feet) and was cut down by mortars and heavy machinegun fire. Several more landing craft missed their entry points but this allowed the remains of B Company to outflank the German defences, destroy the pillboxes and gun emplacements, and advance into the northeast of the

village. To the west, A Company scaled the seawall and entered Bernières under heavy mortar and sniper fire.

At Nan Red, A and B Companies of the North Shore Regiment were dropped in deeper water offshore. The naval bombardment had been ineffective around the village of Saint-Aubin so A Company faced a desperate struggle to the beach and then a sprint across 100 metres (330 feet) of open ground under heavy machinegun fire. Of those who weren't picked off, almost all were accounted for by mines on the beach.

B Company eventually breached the seawall but they couldn't take the 50mm emplacement beyond and it destroyed four tanks. More armour of the Royal Engineers was deployed to the position and the 50mm battery was eventually silenced with anti-tank guns and petard shells. Fifty-two German soldiers were killed in the action and 48 surrendered.

The 8th Brigade's reserve battalion lost half its landing craft to mines at the tide line but B and C Companies then moved in to relieve the beleaguered A Company. They advanced into Saint-Aubin to link up with the Queen's Own Rifles and the North Shores. Then 400 men of No. 48 Royal Marine Commando came ashore to take Langrune-sur-Mer, but positions to the east of Saint-Aubin had not been cleared by the bombardment or the first wave of infantry and they lost 160 men during the landing phase.

Although the reports of battle were mixed, Major-General Rod Keller decided to land more reserves from the 9th Infantry and tanks from the Sherbrooke Fusiliers. Mines continued to be the biggest problem so the entire brigade was sent to Nan White, which had already been cleared. This led to congestion offshore, which the Germans exploited, targeting the stationary landing craft with concentrated mortar and artillery fire.

However, 30,000 troops of the 3rd Infantry eventually fought their way over the seawall and advanced inland against the 21st and 12th Panzer Divisions of the Hitler Youth. Sappers of the 619th Independent Field Company were then deployed to clear the beach and approach roads of any remaining mines so that the advance could continue towards the airfield at Carpiquet. Keller's headquarters, meanwhile, was established in the ruins of Bernières around midday.

FAR LEFT The Canadians come ashore on Juno to light resistance

ABOVE The infantry come ashore at Nan White Sector

The push inland was designed to support the Winnipegs in Courseulles and the North Shore Regiment in Saint-Aubin before advancing to Saint Croix and Banville, the latter being the headquarters of the German 726th Infantry. Winnipeg A and C Company of the Canadian Scottish Regiment then pushed into Saint Croix, but they didn't know that the 726th was preparing to counterattack. At the last moment, C Company spotted the danger and halted the counter-strike before it gained momentum.

Banville was taken early in the afternoon and D Company then secured two bridges across the River Seulles. By now the Regina Rifles had pushed further south to Reviers, although they then came up against the retreating German 736th Grenadiers.

The 8th Brigade had lost men and machinery on the beach, and C Company was still fighting to hold Bernières, so their advance inland was slow by comparison. They were then stopped in their tracks at Beny-sur-Mer by anti-tank weapons, and B Company of the Chaudières lost an entire platoon when a German 88mm shell struck one of their self-propelled guns. It took the unit another two hours to enter Beny-sur-Mer, but, although they had time to regroup, they then had to push

BELOW The Queen's Own Rifles approach the airfield at Carpiquet

south towards their main objective: the airfield.

With Keller having established his command post, he convened a meeting of the commanders of the 8th and 9th Infantry and the 2nd Armored Brigade. Their next objectives were to push into Vaux and Graye-sur-Mer. The advance was supported by another naval bombardment from HMCS Algonquin, which silenced a German bunker. Then their tanks pushed into Tailleville and destroyed more German gun emplacements. But the German defences in the town were linked by tunnels and trenches and they resisted for another seven hours, by which time it was too late to capture important radar positions north of the airfield.

More German resistance slowed the advance in Saint-Aubin and Langrune-sur-Mer, which prevented the Canadians meeting up with the British on Sword and forming a continuous frontline. The small contingent of Royal Marines was held at bay by the 736th Grenadiers with their line of 50mm anti-tank weapons, and by nightfall word came through of a possible counterattack from the 21st Panzer Division. (It would be another two days before the villages were finally in Allied hands.)

The advance may have been slow but the Canadians were still pushing to reach their D-Day objectives. However, more resistance from the 21st Panzers finally slowed their march inland and Lieutenant-General Miles Dempsey ordered forces on Gold, Juno and Sword to hold the line at their intermediate objectives and secure a defensive position against more German counterstrikes.

The 7th Infantry were by then in Creully, the 9th Brigade had pushed to within a few miles of Caen (the furthest inland of any unit on D-Day), and the 8th Brigade had fashioned a defensive stronghold around Columby. German units were not in as good shape: the 716th Infantry was in disarray as its lines had been pierced along a broad front, and although the 21st Panzer counterattack had pushed the British and Canadians back, it couldn't dislodge them from the beaches. Hitler only had one option left: send the elite Lehr and 12th Panzer Divisions north along with the SS Panzer Corps.

Casualty predictions for Juno had been high, with Allied losses expected to be more than 2,000. However, only round 400 men were killed during he landings and push inland. German osses were far greater, with Lieutenant-General Wilhelm Richter estimating hat only 1,600 men of nearly 8,000 vere still capable of fighting by the nd of the day. Around 80% of their rtillery had been disabled or captured, nd three days later they were down to ust 300 men.

The Canadian troops were extremely vell prepared, they were supported by unctioning amphibious tanks, and the esistance during the landings them-elves was – compared with Omaha - relatively light. For these reasons, he landings on Juno are considered strategic success. Had there not veen congestion on the beach due to Keller's eagerness to land the rest of is infantry, bottlenecks in the villages vehind the beaches, and confusion over German counterattacks, he Allies would undoubt-dly have achieved all of he objectives or Juno on D-Day.

LEFT Major Rod Keller addresses Canadian troops on Juno

Chapter 10

Sword

Sword Beach was the easternmost
landing site on the Normandy
coast. It stretched several miles from
Ouistreham to Saint-Aubin-sur-Mer

and was also divided into sectors –
Oboe, Peter, Queen and Roger – that
would be assaulted by men of the
British 3rd Infantry. The ultimate
goal of this division was
to reach and liberate the
historic town of Caen
which was around eight
miles (12km) inland.
It also aimed to join
the Canadians coming
ashore at Juno to form a
solid frontline, as well as
linking up with the 6th
Airborne Division that
had come in by glider
to secure vital roadways
and strategic bridges
across the River Orne
and the Caen Canal.

British forces landing on Queen Red Beach

SWORD

LEFT The landings continue at Sword throughout the day

FAR LEFT The 41st Royal Marine Commandos come ashore at Sword

ABOVE British troops follow one of the amphibious 'DD' tanks inland

The division was bolstered by the addition of the 27th Armoured Brigade, a Special Service Brigade containing French commandos, a substantial Royal Marine contingent and elements of the 79th Armoured Division.

At three o'clock in the morning on June 6th, the aerial bombardment began at Sword Beach. A little later, the navy opened up to pound the remaining German defences. By 0730 British infantrymen were pouring ashore at

Peter and Queen with little resistance. The 6th Airborne had already destroyed the artillery battery at Merville so there was little shelling. By 0815, the commando units had cleared the beach and were pushing inland towards the Orne.

The German army was a formidable force but it had been weakened by the disastrous campaign in Russia, as well as being stretched in Italy and North Africa. Many units had been withdrawn from the Eastern Front and were now based in Normandy, primarily to recuperate. Where divisions were

BELOW A Panzer of the 21st Armoured Division prepares to counterattack at Sword

lacking in numbers, they drafted in Eastern European conscripts who were poorly trained and had little motivation to fight the Allies. Despite these perceived weaknesses, Wilhelm Richter could still call upon 8,000 men of the 716th Infantry. There were another four battalions of the 352nd Infantry defending the beach itself and 16,000 men of the 21st Panzer Grenadiers could move north from their positions defending the bridges at a moment's notice.

The defences at Sword Beach had been upgraded in early 1944 as a response to the threat of invasion. There were 20 armoured fortifications, a network of trenches and small-arms nests lining the beach, and the tide line was peppered with smaller obstacles: wooden stakes, anti-personnel mines and hedgehogs. The largest reinforced bunker held eight anti-tank guns, four 75mm cannon and an 88mm howitzer. The beach exits were also heavily fortified, while another six batteries held four 100mm and ten 155mm guns.

With Lieutenant-General Miles Dempsey's men already ashore, a second wave of the British 1st Corps under Lieutenant-General John Crocker landed at Hermanville in the Queen Sector. Within an hour their commando units had reached the Orne and joined the paratroopers but, as they fought their way inland, the fighting became much tougher.

The main German counterattack on D-Day – other than the odd guerrilla-style raid – was mounted by the retreating 21st Panzer Division at Sword. British troops hadn't cemented the frontline by linking up with the Canadians at Juno so they were weak on both flanks. The Germans mounted a solid defence of Caen and then repelled the British advance throughout the afternoon. By 2000 the 192nd Panzer Grenadiers had pushed them eight miles (12km) back to the beach at Lion-sur-Mer. Fearing that they would be trapped on the coast, the British ordered an air strike on the Panzers, which, when combined with a ferocious anti-tank assault, knocked out 50 of the advancing tanks.

The Germans then made a crucial tactical error. While they still had the advantage, they could have surrounded the British in the village but 250 gliders happened to pass overhead at that moment. Thinking they would be surrounded by the 6th Airborne instead, the Germans abandoned their positions.

Nearly 30,000 men came ashore on Sword Beach (bringing the total on D-Day to around 155,000) for the loss of only 683. With the counterattack repelled, the bulk of this force moved inland towards Caen. On June 7th the British finally linked up with the Canadians from Juno but, despite circling Caen and launching several attacks on the city, the 21st Panzergrenadiers held firm. As the attacks continued into the following week, the German defence began to falter but they wouldn't achieve their main objective – capturing Caen – for another month.

BELOW Infantry and tanks hit the beach

Chapter 11

Victory in Europe

Although the Allies established beachheads on all five landing zones, a mix of poor communication, missed landings, scattered airborne paratroopers, heavy German resistance and unpredictable weather denied them many of their secondary and tertiary objectives.

The 82nd and 101st Airborne had suffered heavy casualties after most missed their drop zones in the poor weather, although they had captured Saint-Mère-Église in the west and were gathering themselves into larger groups. The American 4th Division on Utah had come ashore against light resistance and had established a foothold inland by the end of the opening day. Their forces on Omaha, however, had encountered extremely heavy resistance and had taken a huge number of casualties while securing the beach exits against the elite German troops of the 352nd Division. A wave of reinforcements only allowed them to push a mile inland.

On Gold Beach, the British 50th Infantry encountered much lighter resistance and they were able to push inland to link up with Juno (but not with Omaha as had been expected). The Canadians on Juno had a mixed day in that they overcame stern resistance to move inland but they couldn't quite reach all of their objectives because the German 21st Panzers kept them at bay.

The British 3rd Infantry on Sword also established a firm beachhead, but the 21st Panzers prevented them from reaching Caen and linking up with the

Canadians on Juno. This counterattack was meant to oust the British from the beach, but reinforcements from the 6th Airborne were eventually able to force the 21st Panzers to withdraw.

German defences were also confused by the missed Allied landings as it forced them to spread their troops thinly. Also, only Hitler could give the order to deploy Panzer Divisions, so their response was often slow and disorganized. Indeed, the elite Panzer Divisions were only given the order to advance on the beaches at mid afternoon, much too late to halt the Allied advance.

Overall, the landings were a success. Not all of the initial objectives were achieved but, in the coming weeks, the beachheads were secure, Allied forces had linked up and were pushing inland, and the spirited German defence had been broken.

ABOVE An ammunition carrier explodes after being struck by a German mortar during the Battle for Caen

ABOVE Royal Engineers search the ruins of Caen for mines

FAR RIGHT Parisians welcome the liberating Allied forces in August 1944

By the middle of June, most of the units were established inland and they then began the long, slow push east towards Germany. On the Eastern Front, the Red Army had also been enjoying notable successes. Earlier in the year they'd finally liberated Leningrad after the longest siege in military history. They then took the Crimea and Ukraine, although they couldn't overcome Army Group North in Estonia. On 22nd June, however, they launched a huge offensive in Belarus that resulted in the almost complete destruction of Army Group Centre. They then advanced into Romania and Bulgaria where local troops joined the fight against the Nazis. Yugoslavia, Greece and Albania followed, although Hungary only fell with the liberation of Budapest in February 1945, but by then German forces in the east were in full retreat.

VICTORY IN EUROPE

In the west, Paris was liberated by Allied and French Resistance troops on 25th August, but a major airborne assault into the Netherlands was unsuccessful so they continued pushing into Germany from the south. German tanks launched a massive counterattack in the Ardennes Forest in December 1944 but their objectives – capturing Antwerp and splitting the Allied lines – were not achieved and they pulled back in January. In February, the Allies entered Germany and pushed east towards the Rhine while the Red Army drove through Poland, Silesia and Pomerania. The noose was tightening around Hitler's neck as the war entered its end game.

Having taken Budapest and repelled several German counterattacks, the Red Army marched into Austria in March

1945. The Wehrmacht had lost more than a million men and countless artillery weapons and tanks defending the Eastern Front the previous year and they were no longer in a position to defend the Reich. Vienna fell on 13th April and the Russians then pushed into Germany itself.

Hitler appointed master defensive technician General Gotthard Heinrici as Commander-in-Chief of Army Group Vistula and tasked him with defending Berlin. Heinrici flooded the Oder River by releasing water from a reservoir and built three armour belts, including anti-tank ditches and bunkers, around Berlin.

The Russians had been bolstered by the arrival of the 2nd Belorussian Front and they now moved into the Seelow Heights, the last major defensive line around Berlin. After four days of heavy fighting in mid-April, and with the loss of 12,000 men, the German lines were breached. Stalin now ordered one prong to join up with American forces on the banks of the Elbe in the

ABOVE German defenders dig in before the crucial battle at Seelow Heights

south while two more surrounded the remains of the German 9th Army and thrust into Berlin.

On 20th April, the 1st Belorussian Front began bombarding Berlin and they didn't stop until they'd fired more ordnance into the city than that dropped by British and American bombers in the previous five years. By 25th April,

Berlin was completely surrounded but, to avoid friendly fire casualties, the Allies held their positions and allowed Soviet forces to enter the city.

By now Hitler knew the war was lost. He'd already berated his generals for their incompetence and treachery and vowed to shoot himself before the Russians could take him. Despite his

acceptance of defeat, however, he knew he could still call upon 40,000 regular troops and about the same number of police, Hitler Youth and World War One veterans.

Stalin, on the other hand, had more than a million men under his command and they advanced into the city centre along the Frankfurter Allee, Sonnen Allee and Potsdamer Platz, and from the north towards the Reichstag. The heaviest fighting was centred around the Moltke Bridge, Alexanderplatz and Havel Bridge but the Red Army soon had a foothold in the city centre.

With Soviet forces closing in on the Reichstag, General Helmuth Weilding realised his only chance of escape lay in abandoning their positions and trying to slip through the Russian lines. Only Hitler could approve the plan but he refused to surrender at a subsequent meeting. Outside, the Russian tanks gave way to General Zhukov's infantry for the final assault on the parliament building 200 metres (660 feet) from Hitler's bunker. Despite meeting fierce resistance from the SS on the upper levels, they fought their way inside and eventually captured the Reichstag on the morning of 30th April 1945.

The Führer then summoned his private adjutant, Otto Günsche, to his chamber. Hitler explained that his staff had failed him and the Red Army would soon overrun their positions. He instructed Günsche to get a can of petrol so that his body could be burned instead of exhibited after his death. He

BELOW German tanks make a last stand

ABOVE Berlin lies in ruins

then lined his staff up to thank them before giving Weilding permission to try to escape and then returning to his private quarters. Günsche waited outside for 15 minutes before Martin Bormann entered to confirm that Hitler and Eva Braun had killed themselves. The bodies were removed by his valet, Heinz Linge, and taken via an emergency exit to the garden of the Reich Chancellery where they were repeatedly doused with petrol and burned. The remains, along with those of Hitler's two dogs, the entire Goebbels family

and General Hans Krebs, were discovered by the Red Army in a shell crater and removed shortly afterwards.

(The remains were apparently repeatedly buried and exhumed before being loaded in wooden boxes and shipped to Magdeburg. These were then cremated in 1970 and the ashes scattered in the Biederitz River, although a fragment of the jawbone and part of the skull with a bullet hole were preserved. Recent DNA tests have cast doubt on their authenticity, however, with the skull appearing to be that of a woman in her 30s.)

Hitler's remaining generals begged for peace and the war in Europe was declared over on 7th May. The treaty was signed in Berlin the following day, although the remains of Germany's Army Group Centre held out in Prague until May 11th.

Under the terms of the agreement, Austria was declared a neutral state, while Germany was divided up into zones of administration under British, American, Polish, French and Russian control. The boundaries agreed by the Allies were difficult to police, however, and there were feelings of resentment and anger across the continent. There were also deep suspicions in the West about Stalin's motives and goals, and Europe was soon divided again. In the east, the Warsaw Pact saw Poland, East Germany, the Baltic States, Czechoslovakia, Romania and Albania become Soviet satellites with unpopular communist regimes. West Germany and West Berlin came under the protection of NATO, however, which only heightened the tension in central Europe and led to the Cold War.

ABOVE The Reichstag parliament building shows signs of wear and tear after heavy fighting between the Russians and Germans

Chapter 12

A Wider Peace

By 1945, the war in the Pacific was in its fourth year. The conflict had turned into a brutal and bloody arm-wrestle for outposts like the Mariana Islands, Iwo Jima, Midway, Okinawa and the Philippines. With most of the outlying islands secure by June 1945, preparations were well underway for the invasion of Japan under the code-name Operation Downfall.

This invasion was planned in two parts. The first, Operation Olympic, would begin in October and involved landing the US 6th Army with the intention of taking the southern end of the island of Ky sh . In March 1946, Operation Coronet would see the 1st, 8th and 10th Armies take the Kant plain near Tokyo on the island of Honsh .

The Japanese had plenty of time to prepare for the invasion and could mobilise more than two million front-line troops and four million reservists, plus there was also a civilian militia of 28 million. With the US having taken Okinawa, both sides learned from the engagement and predicted enormous casualties on both sides if the US were to invade the mainland. Up to 20 million Japanese civilians and military personnel, and at least a million Allied soldiers, would die during the endgame.

These figures were so high that the Allies were forced to rethink their strategy for ending the war. They began a massive firebombing campaign that destroyed several cities, but that only seemed to make the Japanese more resilient and they began stockpiling

munitions to repel the invasion. (On the night of 9th March 1945, an estimated 100,000 Japanese were killed during the firebombing of Tokyo.) The Allies even contemplated using poison gas but opted instead to drop leaflets urging the Japanese to surrender lest they be completely annihilated.

ABOVE The result of the firebombing campaign on Tokyo

ABOVE American B-29 Superfortresses drop incendiary bombs on Yokohama in 1945

FAR RIGHT Another image of the terrible damage inflicted on Toky by the firebombing

With Japan refusing to admit defeat and accept unconditional surrender, however, President Truman was forced to contemplate invading. But he was also facing pressure from the public to end the war and bring their troops home so he asked Prime Minister Clement Attlee if he was right to use the weapon they'd jointly been developing that could end the war immediately. Attlee agreed that the atomic bomb should be used as a military and political weapon, the latter to dissuade Stalin from making further advances in the Far East.

On 5th August 1945, Truman issued an order to the 509th Composite Group on Tinian Island in the Marianas. Their mission was to drop Little Boy, a uranium bomb, on Hiroshima the following day. Colonel Paul Tibbets had been training for the run with modified B-29s for three months but his crew still wasn't prepared for the news that the new bomb would carry the power of around 15,000 tons of TNT. (The largest conventional bomb dropped in the war was the Barnes Wallis-designed five-ton Tallboy, which only carried two tons of explosive.)

Early on the morning of 6th August, the B-29, christened Enola Gay after Tibbets's mother, took off from Tinian and headed north towards Japan. She was accompanied by observation and instrumentation aircraft that would document the results. By 0730, the bomb was armed so Tibbets climbed to 30,000 feet. He then received confirmation from a meteorological aircraft ahead of them that Hiroshima, their primary target, a city that had swollen to around 300,000 people after the fire bombing of other towns, was visible beneath scattered cloud.

The first aircraft was spotted from

the ground and an air-raid alert was sounded across the city, but it was lifted when radar confirmed there were only a few planes, which the Japanese believed to be reconnaissance aircraft.

In the belly of the Enola Gay, bombardier Thomas Ferebee spotted the T-shaped Aioi Bridge spanning the Ota River and dropped the bomb at 0915. Forty-three seconds later it detonated at around 2,000 feet above the city centre. An estimated 80,000 people were killed instantly in the 15-million-degree fireball, including 20,000 military personnel. About the same number were injured, mostly blinded by the light or burnt by the horrific heat, although both numbers would rise significantly due to radiation poisoning. More than two thirds of the population would eventually succumb to the bomb, and around 70% of the city's buildings were destroyed.

The Enola Gay was struck by several shockwaves but she had already swung round and was heading for Okinawa. When the aircraft finally made it back to Tinian, the crew was decorated and enjoyed a welcome-home party.

Later that day, General Leslie Groves, director of the Manhattan project that produced the bomb, contacted Doctor Robert Oppenheimer to congratulate him on his creation. But Oppenheimer, having heard about the enormous destruction, was unsure about the ethical implications of deploying such a weapon and many of his team were concerned that it could lead to retaliatory strikes in the future.

President Truman learned of the outcome while returning to the United States from the Potsdam Conference on the USS Augusta. He was said to be pleased with the results and sent yet another ultimatum to the Japanese: surrender or face more of the same. The Japanese saw things differently, however, because with all communications down and the city largely destroyed, they could not appreciate the scale of the disaster. Accurate reports did not reach Emperor Hirohito for at least 36 hours and he still refused to surrender. In fact he then asked Stalin for help.

On 8th August, Japanese Foreign Minister Shigenori T g was authorised to contact the Russians and ask them to mediate a proposed peace deal between Japan and the Allies. But Stalin refused: he was concerned that the balance of power had shifted to the west and he

FAR LEFT The first atomic bomb strikes Hiroshima

knew that the Americans wouldn't hesitate to use another nuclear weapon. He responded by declaring war on the Japanese in the hope that he could further his imperial pretensions in the Far East.

The following morning the Russians launched Operation August Storm against the Japanese along the Manchurian border with over a million troops, 5,000 tanks and 26,000 field guns. The weary Japanese were overwhelmed and Soviet forces moved into North Korea.

President Truman was immediately concerned that Stalin would try to occupy strategic territory in Korea, Japan and throughout the Far East. He'd already claimed much of Eastern Europe and suspicions were running high. Truman knew he had to act quickly if he was going to stop Stalin claiming more territory in the region but he was faced with a dilemma: welcome the Soviet Union into the war and see them overrun the mainland, or temper that welcome with a warning to stay clear of American interests. He chose the latter to show Stalin he meant business and had the technological know-how to win any future conflict, so he authorised the use of a second atomic bomb: Fat Man.

The mission was brought forward two days and the device was loaded onto a second B-29 nicknamed Bockscar. Major Charles Sweeney swapped aircraft with Captain Frederick Bock at the last moment and took command for the flight to Kokura, home to a massive military arsenal on the northern tip of Ky sh . In the event of poor weather over the target, the secondary objective would be the industrial town of Nagasaki.

Bockscar took off from Tinian in the early hours of 9th August in the middle of a tropical storm. It was then discovered that the aircraft had a faulty fuel pump so Sweeney had to climb above the storm to conserve fuel. By midmorning they were above Kokura but cloud and smog obscured the target, so, after three runs across the city, which used up valuable fuel, they aborted and headed for Nagasaki.

Sweeney knew that if Nagasaki was also obscured by cloud he was in real trouble because they didn't have enough fuel to carry a five-ton bomb to the nearest friendly airbase on Okinawa. When the aircraft arrived at Nagasaki, the city was also covered with cloud

so the crew decided to go for a radar-guided drop, but a brief gap opened up at just after eleven in the morning. Bombardier Captain Kermit Beahan dropped the plutonium implosion device halfway between the Mitsubishi Steel & Arms Works in the south and the Ordnance Works in the north.

At 22 kilotons, the yield was considerably higher than Little Boy but part of the city was protected by hills. Despite this, the 4,000-degree heat and 1,000km/h winds killed up to 60,000 people instantly, with at least another 20,000 succumbing to injuries and radiation poisoning by the end of the year.

If the Japanese chose to fight on by adhering to the principles of total war, one city after another would be erased so Emperor Hirohito was left with no option but to urge the supreme war council to admit defeat and surrender. The Imperial High Command couldn't agree on the terms, however, so the Allies resumed their conventional bombing campaign against strategic military targets. On 12th August, Hirohito informed the imperial family of his decision to accept the terms of the Potsdam Treaty and surrendered, providing he remained on the throne.

But US Secretary of State James Burns refused to accept this condition and said that everyone in Japan would be treated equally by General Douglas MacArthur. Burns even suggested trying the emperor as a war criminal and sentencing him to death if he was found guilty. MacArthur appreciated how important the role of the emperor was to the Japanese people and was outraged at such a suggestion. It was one thing to defeat an enemy in battle but to humiliate them afterwards was unacceptable.

The Allied terms were amended so that the Japanese throne would be preserved and Hirohito delivered his capitulation announcement on 15th August. There was extra pressure to sign the agreement because the Soviet Union was now within striking distance of Japan and communism and the emperor system were totally incompatible. The only way to ensure their traditional way of life therefore was to reach the agreement solely with the Americans. There was a brief rebellion by loyal troops opposed to the surrender but it soon petered out. Two weeks later the agreement was formally signed aboard the USS Missouri.

FAR LEFT Mamoru Shigemitsu signs the Japanese instrument of surrender aboard the USS Missouri on September 2nd 1945

There was initial delight at the way the atomic bombs had ended the war so quickly, but reports from Japan – especially those containing photographs of the damage and human casualties from ground zero in both cities – were heavily censored. When the full horror of the atomic holocaust finally became known there was an upsurge in hostility towards using weapons of this kind.

The bombs may have brought about the end of the war but at what cost? It's difficult to assess but on Okinawa and Iwo Jima more than 95% of the Japanese defenders were killed because they refused to surrender. If the same happened on the main islands of Japan, casualty figures would have run into the millions, certainly more than the 250,000 killed by the bombs.

Others argue that by stepping up the firebombing campaign, and with Stalin having torn up his alliance with Japan and advancing through Korea, it was only a matter of time before Hirohito surrendered anyway. It seemed an invasion of Japan was now a viable option because with Stalin onside troop casualties would be minimised. Truman even noted in his diary that from 15th August onwards, the Soviet Union would have

entered the war against Japan. This now became Truman's deadline because he was desperate to end the war without Stalin's help lest the latter continue his aggressive seizure of land in Eastern Europe and the Far East. The Soviet Union had been ravaged by war and the loss of 20 million men but it was recovering fast and was growing powerful, too powerful for Truman's liking.

We will never know if dropping the bombs was ethically or morally correct, or if lives were saved in the long-term, but we do know that they contributed to ending the bloodiest war in history.

Although casualty figures are unreliable because deaths were not recorded accurately, it is estimated that 60 million people died during the war, most from genocide, disease and starvation rather than in battle. The Soviet Union bore the brunt of the horrors but eight million Chinese died during the Japanese occupation and six million Jews were exterminated by the Germans in the holocaust in Eastern Europe.

Although the economies of the US, West Germany, France and Japan recovered quickly, Britain remained mired in depression for nearly two dec-

ades and the overall cost of the war is impossible to calculate.

The German High Command were rounded up and sent to trial for war crimes at the Palace of Justice in Nuremburg. The first of these tried 23 political and military leaders of the Third Reich, although Hitler, Himmler and Goebbels had all committed suicide by then and Martin Bormann was almost certainly dead. Those found guilty were sentenced to death by hanging.

None of the Allies were tried for war crimes despite various accusations of brutality against the occupying forces in Germany.

ABOVE The author's grandfather, Group Captain James Warne, accepts the Japanese Sword of Surrender on Bali. Warne flew sorties for RAF Bomber Command throughout the war, and he bombed the port of Le Havre in Northern France on D-Day

The images in this book have been provided courtesy of the following.:

WIKIMEDIA COMMONS

Design & Artwork: ALEX YOUNG

Published by: DEMAND MEDIA LIMITED

Publisher: JASON FENWICK

Written by: LIAM McCANN